Supporting
Family Literacy & Lifelong
Learning

Ontario   Culture Ministry of

The Honourable Caroline Di Cocco,

Minister of Culture

announces Literacy Grant

through Ontario Government under

Premier Dalton McGuinty

Enhancing the vital role of Ontario's libraries
as community hubs of literacy and learning

discovering **nature**

Your Backyard

Sally Hewitt

Copper Beech Books
Brookfield, Connecticut

© Aladdin Books Ltd 2000

Designed and produced by
Aladdin Books Ltd
28 Percy Street
London W1P OLD

First published in the United States
in 2000 by
Copper Beech Books,
an imprint of
The Millbrook Press
2 Old New Milford Road
Brookfield, Connecticut 06804

Editor: Kathy Gemmell

Consultant: Helen Taylor

Designer: Simon Morse

Photography: Roger Vlitos

Illustrators: Tony Kenyon, Stuart Squires – SGA
& Mike Atkinson

Printed in Belgium

Cataloging-in-Publication Data is on file at the Library of Congress

ISBN 0-7613-1157-2 (lib. bdg.)

Orginal design concept by David West Children's Books.

Contents

Introduction

Look closely and you will find many interesting things in your backyard. You can have fun learning about creatures and where to find them. Make a worm garden and watch worms at work in the soil. Plot an ant map and attract birds with a cake. See what plants need in order to grow and find out who visits the yard when you're not there.

1 Look out for numbers like this. They will guide you through the step-by-step instructions for the projects and activities, making sure that you do things in the right order.

Further facts

Whenever you see this "nature spotters" sign, you will find interesting information, such as how to recognize animal footprints, to help you understand more about your backyard.

Hints and tips

• When you look for things in the yard, be careful not to step on any plants.

• Try to look at creatures without disturbing them. If you do move them, always return them to the place where you found them.

• Before touching soil, always cover any cuts you may have with a bandage.

• Do not rub your face or eyes when working with plants or soil. Always wash your hands afterward.

DON'T TOUCH ROTTEN THINGS

Wherever you see this sign, ask an adult to help you. Never use sharp tools or go exploring by yourself.

Get an adult to help you

This warning sign shows where you have to take special care when doing the project. For example, when looking at trash rotting in bags of soil, keep the bags sealed. Don't touch or smell the rotten things. They may give you germs that make you ill.

Soil

Soil is a very important part of your backyard. It is full of the minerals and water that plants need for growth. Moles, worms, and all kinds of tiny creatures make it their home.

Soil settling

1 Find out what makes up the soil in your backyard. Dig up some soil from the edge of a flower bed and put it in a bucket.

2 Shake some soil in a sieve over the bucket. Sort what is left behind onto some paper. You may find stones, bits of plants, or even creatures that live in the soil.

3 Now put some soil into a screw-top jar. Fill the jar nearly to the top with water and screw on the lid.

4 Shake the soil and water together, then leave the jar to stand.

5 Carefully look at the jar without disturbing it. The soil will settle into layers in the water.

Soil layers

Soil is a mixture of dead plants and animals and tiny pieces of broken-down rock. Different kinds of rock will make sandy, chalky, or sticky clay soil.

Bits of plants

Muddy water

Clay or chalk

Sand

Gravel and stones

Rotting garbage

Dead plants and animals that rot down into the soil help to make it rich and good for new plants to grow in. Not everything rots down quickly. Some garbage stays around for a very long time.

Bags of garbage

1 See what kind of garbage rots away, and what doesn't. Don't throw away banana skins, apple cores, tissues, cans, or potato chip bags - bury them!

NEVER TAKE GARBAGE FROM THE CAN

2 Put some soil into clear plastic bags. Push one piece of garbage into the soil in each bag and seal it.

3 Check the bags every few days, but don't open them. You will see that apple cores rot quickly, but banana skins take a long time. Garbage made of plastic doesn't rot at all.

Natural rotters

There are many different plants and animals that get to work right away on natural garbage like leaves, logs, or dead creatures. They are called decomposers.

Fungi are not really plants. They grow and feed on dead wood.

Lichens grow on stone and wood and gradually break them down.

Worms pull leaves and bits of dead plant down into the soil and eat them.

Maggots that hatch from housefly eggs eat the bodies of dead creatures.

Woodlice live in dark, damp places and feed on leaves and wood.

Seeds

Gardeners look after the plants and flowers they want to grow in their yards, and spend a lot of time pulling up weeds that they didn't plant. You can discover what seeds are hiding in the soil, waiting to grow.

Soil gardens

1 Dig up some soil from two different places in the yard, perhaps from under a tree and by a fence. Put the soil from each place in its own plastic tray and label where it came from.

2 Water both trays every other day. After a while, you will see shoots beginning to push up through the soil even though you didn't plant any seeds.

3 Some shoots may become grass or weeds. A seed from a tree may one day grow into a young tree. A rose tree may even grow from a rose hip dropped by a bird.

Spreading seeds

Plants have various ways of spreading their seeds to give them a good chance to grow into new, strong plants.

Birds eat juicy fruits, such as cherries. The seeds or pits inside them fall to the ground in the birds' droppings.

Horse chestnut seeds are heavy and fall straight to to the ground. Look for them under a horse chestnut tree.

Dandelion seeds float on little parachutes. The wind can blow the seeds far and wide.

Green grass

Grass in the countryside is food for animals and it can be like a soft, green carpet in the yard. Grass has another job to do, too.

Grass roots hold soil in place in the wind and the rain. Different kinds of grass grow in different soils.

In the dark

1 This project will show you that sunlight is what makes grass green. Find a corner of your lawn.

2 Cover a patch of grass, near the edge of the lawn, with a thick piece of cardboard. Put a stone on it to stop it blowing away.

3 Lift up the cardboard after two weeks and see what has happened to the grass. When kept in the dark, grass will turn pale green or yellow and begin to die.

Using sunlight

Like grass, other plants also need sunlight to grow and survive. Plants make their own food using sunlight. This is called photosynthesis.

Photosynthesis

Plants need sunlight to make food using the green color in their leaves, called chlorophyll.

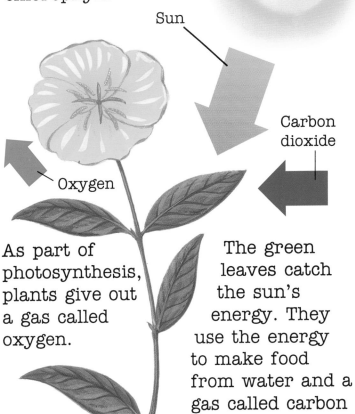

Sun

Carbon dioxide

Oxygen

As part of photosynthesis, plants give out a gas called oxygen.

The green leaves catch the sun's energy. They use the energy to make food from water and a gas called carbon dioxide in the air.

Without sunlight, plants cannot make food and they will die.

Plants

We all have veins to carry blood around our bodies. Plants have veins, too. They carry the water and minera a plant needs to grow to every part of the plant. Watch how water moves up the stem and into the leaves of a celery stalk.

Drinking water

1 For this project you will need a jar of water, some blue food coloring, and a celery stalk with leaves.

2 Mix the water and blue food coloring together in the jar and put the celery stalk in it. Leave the jar near a window for a few hours.

3 The blue water will slowly rise up the veins in the stalk, then into the leaves, turning them blue.

Get an adult to help you

4 Now slice the stalk across the middle. You will be able to see that the veins in the celery have been stained blue.

Roots

Roots grow downward into the soil to hold the plant in place. They have tiny hairs to suck up the water and minerals that a plant needs from the soil. Water goes into the roots, then up the stem into the leaves, then out into the air.

Carrots and potatoes are swollen roots that store food for the plants.

Water in the soil

Flowers

A plant starts life as a tiny egg. Flowers are the parts of a plant where eggs that become seeds are made. The seeds then grow into new plants. If you look closely at a flower, you will see all the parts it needs for making seeds.

Ovary

Stem

Petal

Parts of a flower

1 Stamens grow from the middle of the flower. Yellow powder called pollen is made on the tip of the stamens. Pollen gives some people hayfever.

Pollen

Stamen

2 Petals use colors, smells, and patterns to attract insects and birds that feed on pollen and on a sweet juice made by the plant, called nectar.

Stamen

3 A stigma also grows from the middle of the flower. Pollen grains that land on the stigma grow a tube down to join an egg in the ovary. The egg can then become a seed.

4 The ovary is the case where eggs that become seeds are made.

From stigma

Ovary

Pollen fertilizes an egg to make a seed.

Flower power

Look for flowers of all colors, shapes, sizes, and smells growing in different places in the yard.

Apple blossom

Apple blossoms on an apple tree become fruit in the summer.

Daffodil bulbs can be planted in pots and window boxes.

Daffodil

Honeysuckle grows up walls and fences. It smells very sweet.

Honeysuckle

Stigma

Birds

Birds are visitors to the yard, looking for food and water. In the spring, they may find a sheltered place there to build a nest. You can make sure there is always something for birds to eat and drink.

Winter bird cake

1 In winter, there is less food for birds to find. Use breadcrumbs from a stale loaf, uncooked peanuts, bacon rind, and fat to make a winter bird cake.

2 Line a cake pan or muffin tray with wax paper. Now mix the breadcrumbs, peanuts, and chopped bacon rind together in a bowl.

3 Fat will hold the cake together as well as keep the birds warm when they eat it. Melt the fat in a saucepan over a low heat until it is all liquid.

Get an adult to help you

5 Let the mixture cool. Then turn it out of the tray and put your winter cake outside, out of reach of cats. Put out water, too.

4 Stir the melted fat into the dry mixture and pour it into the cake pan or muffin tray.

Bird food

Birds will find things to eat all over the yard.

Some birds feed on berries and fruit. Some catch insects in the air.

Caterpillars, snails, and worms make a juicy meal.

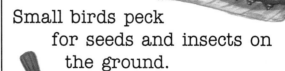

Small birds peck for seeds and insects on the ground.

In winter, when the ground is hard and there are no berries, birds will eat your winter cake.

Footprints

Birds are not the only visitors to the backyard who come looking for food and water. Other shy creatures come at night or when there is no one around. Their footprints will let you know who visited.

Hungry visitors

1 Fill a baking tray with damp sand and smooth it over. Put food scraps like brown bread, fruit, vegetables, and nuts on a plate. Pour milk or water into a saucer.

2 Put the food and liquid onto the baking tray and leave it in a quiet part of the yard. Check the tray for footprints in the morning and again in the evening.

3 Make a note of who has left tracks in the sand. Did they come at night or during the day? Look carefully, then smooth over the sand

Identifying tracks

You can use these pictures to identify the footprints that have been made in your tray. These pictures are the same size as real animal footprints.

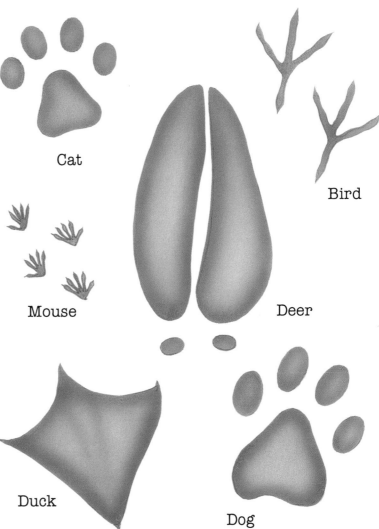

Cat

Bird

Mouse

Deer

Duck

Dog

If you can't see a print to match the ones in your tray, try to find the one that looks most like it. Can you tell if it is a bird or an animal? Is it big or small? Ask an adult to help you work out what any mystery prints are. You could look them up in a field guide.

Insects

Look for insects in the soil, under stones, on plants, resting on walls, hiding in cracks, or swimming in water. Make a chart of the insects that live in or visit the backyard.

Insect visitors

1 You will need a sheet of cardboard, a ruler, colored markers, and a magnifying glass.

2 Copy the chart in the picture onto your cardboard. You can add extra columns. Draw a moon if you spot an insect like a moth at night.

Where insects live

Dragonfly

	Ladybug	Wasp	Butterfly
			x
		x	

DON'T GO TOO CLOSE TO WASPS AND BEES

3 Look for insects in the backyard. Mark a cross on the chart to show what they are feeding on. What part of the yard has the most visitors? Do the insects come during the day or at night?

A bug's parts

Insects all have six legs. They have a skeleton on the outside of their bodies and sensitive feelers called antennae. Many have wings.

Wasp

Thorax

Wing

Abdomen

Leg

Antenna

Compound eye

Insects can look very different from each other. Beetles have hard, shiny cases to protect their delicate wings. The easiest way to tell if a creature is an insect is to count its legs.

Beetle

Minibeasts

There are many small creatures, such as spiders and slugs, that are not insects. Spiders spin silky webs to catch their food. Slugs and snails slither along on silvery trails. Millipedes scuttle in dark, damp places. Set a trap to catch some minibeasts in your backyard.

Setting a trap

1 Dig a hole in the soil just deep enough to hold a small container. Put in pieces of fruit and a spoonful of cat food or dog food.

2 Cover the trap with a small rock, propping up one end with a stone to leave a small gap.

3 Leave the trap overnight. Lift the rock to see what you have caught. Before you let your minibeasts go, try to find out what they are.

Minibeast spotting

Use a magnifying glass and see if you can spot some of these creatures in your backyard.

A snail hides inside its shell when it is in danger.

Snail

Spiders are not insects because they have eight legs.

Spider

Millipedes, with hundreds of legs, eat leaves and dead plants.

Millipede

Slugs come out to look for food after rain.

Slug

Ants

Ants have six legs, so you know they are insects. Ants often move around in long trails, following the same path. This project will help you find out if there is a busy ants' nest in your backyard.

Bait

Bait

Nest

Bai

Ant trails

1 Mix two teaspoons of sugar in a bowl half filled with warm water. Stir until the sugar dissolves.

2 Add small pieces of stale bread and leave them to soak for a few moments. Remove the bread before it gets too soggy and take it into the yard.

3 Put pieces of bread all over the yard as bait. Ants will find the food and carry it off, moving in a line. If you follow the line, you will find the ants' nest.

4 Draw a map of where you put the bread bait. Put in lines to show the paths the ants took to carry their food. The nest should be where all the lines meet.

Bait

Bait

Ants' nests

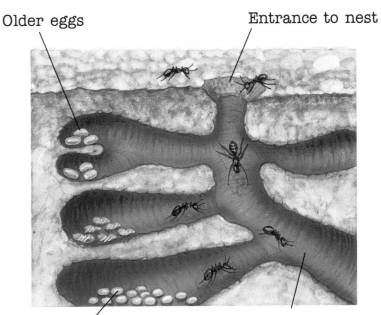

Ants live and work together in a nest underground. They build lots of tunnels. A queen ant lays eggs. Worker ants look for food and bring it back home along the tunnels.

Older eggs

Entrance to nest

Young eggs

Main tunnel

Worms

As worms burrow along under the ground, they eat soil, leaving behind mounds of fine soil called worm casts. You can watch worms pull leaves and dead plants down into the soil to munch.

Worm watching

1 You will need a shoe box, a plastic trash bag, plastic wrap, leaves, tape, dead plants, soil, and worms.

2 Line the box with the plastic trash bag and secure it in place with tape. This will make the box waterproof.

3 Fill the box with damp soil and put in some worms you have dug up from the soil in the yard.

4 Let the worms burrow down into the soil, then sprinkle on the plants and leaves.

5 Cover the box with plastic wrap punched with holes to let in air. How long does it take for the leaves and plants to disappear?

Words on worms

Worms are not garden pests. Gardeners are very happy to have worms in the soil because they help to break it up. Breaking up the soil keeps it full of air, which is good for growing plants. Soil without any worms in it is solid, very heavy to dig, and not as good for growing things.

Glossary

Ants

Ants are insects that live in a nest underground. They carry food away in long trails.

Turn to pages 26-27 to find out how you can lay a food trail to see if there is an ants' nest in the backyard.

Birds

Birds feed on berries and fruit, or insects and creatures they find on the ground. In winter, it is hard for them to find enough to eat.

You can learn how to make a winter bird cake on pages 18-19.

Decomposers

Decomposers are creatures or plants that help dead animals and plants to break down, or decompose.

You can find out how long different objects take to decompose in the project on pages 8-9.

Flowers

Flowers are where the seeds for new plants are made. They come in all shapes and sizes, but all have the same parts.

Find out what the parts of a flower are on pages 16-17.

Grass

Grass holds the soil in place and provides food for animals. Grass needs sunlight to stay green.

See how to prove that grass needs sunlight to stay green on pages 12-13.

Insects

All insects have six legs. Any creature with more or less than six legs is not an insect. Different insects like to feed in different places.

Chart the best places to spot insects in the yard, and look at the parts that make up an insect on pages 22-23.

Photosynthesis

Photosynthesis is the name for the way that plants use sunlight, carbon dioxide, water and the green color in their leaves, called chlorophyll, to make their own food.

Look at how photosynthesis works on pages 12-13.

Roots

Roots hold plants firmly in the ground. Water and minerals from the soil go up through the roots and into the plant.

You can watch how plants use water in the project on pages 14-15, using a celery stick and some colored water.

Seeds

Plants grow from seeds. Inside a seed is a new plant and the food that it needs to begin to grow.

You can discover if there are seeds waiting to grow under the soil in the project on pages 10-11.

Soil

Soil is made up of several layers of rock and dead plants and animals that have been broken down over many years. Different types of rock break down to make different kinds of soil.

You can look at how to shake up soil so that you can see all the layers in the project on pages 6-7.

Worms

Worms live in the soil. They break up the soil and make it easier for plants to grow. Most gardeners like to have worms in their soil.

You can learn how to build your own worm garden in the project on pages 28-29.

Index